Newbie's Guide to Kink

A BDSM Companion

By

J. Byrd Brown

Copyright 2015

Table of Contents

Introduction

First and foremost, this guide is intended as an overview for the curious beginner, the novice practitioner, and even for helping enlighten the open-minded friend or family member. The presentation of views, ideas, practices, roles, and lifestyles is straightforward, respectful of the sanctity of the Individual, and will, hopefully, be useful to you in genuinely getting to know your own ideas; all the while learning to appreciate, understand, and tolerate the differing ideas of others. Sex is, after all, a healthy practice. One that almost every person engages in and enjoys, at least to some degree. Why not try to maximize that enjoyment by incorporating some creativity, open-mindedness, and acceptance?

If you ask a hundred people to summarize the state of sexuality in the world today, you'll probably get ninety nine distinct answers and one blank look....don't mind that guy. For some, sexuality (i.e., sexual acts, fantasies, ideas, identity) is at the core of a healthy life. For others, it is a private, shameful, secret facet of life that is meant to be acknowledged only behind closed doors and between the hours of 11 P.M. and 2 A.M. Sexuality is one of the most diversely viewed (and felt) aspects of the human experience. It is a powerful and intense part of us.

It is my sincere hope that this presentation will help readers learn to relax and to embrace enjoy your TRUE self; as opposed to the mask that most of us wear in order to influence and cater to the perceptions of others. Some of you may have some pretty dirty secrets that you hide behind your mask. Some unusual ideas, fantasies, desires that you are hiding, denying, or suppressing in order to conform to a particular definition of "normal." Some of you may even be hiding these shamefully secret parts of yourself and your psyche from your significant other. It is to each and every one of you, the keepers of dirty secrets, that this work is dedicated; the ones who worry that sharing those secret thoughts would earn contempt and ridicule from even their closest, trusted partner.

Regardless of what caught your attention and brought you here, to BDSM and kink... Congratulations! Welcome to a wonderfully open, supportive, helpful, and responsible community! Whatever you're into, there are others out there who will value your ideas and opinions. There are social networks to help you find those who understand your way of thinking about all things kinky. There are, of course, dangers and pitfalls. There are also widely held guidelines for personal safety and protecting the rights of others.

Safety

Please understand that safety is always the primary responsibility of every practitioner. We are all entitled to make our own choices and when we consent to engage in an act, of any sort (especially sexual, erotic, intimate, etc.), it should be *informed* consent. There are two popular views in the community that outline a basic plan for safety during any interpersonal exchange:

1) Safe, Sane, and Consensual (SSC)

2) Risk-Aware Consensual Kink (RACK)

The main difference between the two is the contrast in the words "safe" and "risk-aware".

Many of the activities we choose to perform in our daily lives are dangerous; driving on the freeway, smoking, listening to loud music, eating junk food and so on. Some people choose to do things that are dangerous because the experiences add value to the amazing masterpiece of life. Some flirt with danger to feed an addiction. Whatever the reason, being "risk-aware" implies a state that is both more honest with yourself and better informed about possible dangers and negative outcomes.

Some kinky acts are riskier than others. Some people are more responsible than others. When trying something new, it is always best not to rush. Give yourself time to consider the risks, ask questions, do research, and....ask more questions. When interacting with a new person, be sure to have safety protocols in place. Make sure that at least two trusted people know where you are and who you are with. Set a time to check in with someone by phone to verify that you're safe. If this new person is offended by these small inconveniences, that's probably a sign that he/she isn't up for a safe or responsible, risk-aware experience.

BDSM/Kink Overview

BDSM is a four letter abbreviation that encompasses three categories of power exchange behavior:

Bondage and Discipline

Dominance and submission (D/s)

Sadism and Masochism (S&M)

"Kink" is defined as unconventional or non-normative sexual practices, concepts, and fantasies. This is a bit broad and ambiguous, because everyone has a slightly different view of what is conventional or normal. The term is derived from the idea of a "bend" (or kink) in one's sexual identity, or behavior, as opposed to "straight" or "vanilla". The word "kink" is also used by some practitioners as an umbrella term that refers to a spectrum of sexual practices and paraphilias.

Some of the specific roles and most common practices of the kink community will be discussed in more detail later in this book.

Motivation

Why do we "do it kinky?" Why can't we just "do it normal?"

Homo sapiens are a complex bunch. The act of sex is pleasurable for many species, but human beings have a tendency to "go big or go home." Humans are sexually aroused on the physical and psychological levels independently, which differentiates us from most other species.

Within the Physical and Psychological, there are numerous factors that work (or sometimes fail to work) to create various levels of arousal and motivation.

Physical Factors

Neurochemicals - A neurochemical is an organic molecule that participates in neural activity; e.g., serotonin, dopamine, endocannabinoids, oxytocin, endorphins, GABA, adrenaline and various others. Each of these neurochemicals is associated with one or two prominent physiological effects.

Brain Structure- Human beings share some aspects of brain structure with other mammals, such as rats and apes. One of these commonalities, a group of structures collectively called the Limbic system, plays an integral part in human sexuality.

During arousal and sexual activity, neurochemical changes take place in the limbic system. This is considered a "primitive" part of the human brain (in contrast to the brain structures associated with higher reasoning and abstract thought) and is the seat of drives, impulses, and desires; including sexual desires. The job of the limbic system is to keep you alive and reproducing. One could debate its role in falling in love (this is the area responsible for basic emotions such as fear, anger, and pleasure), but it is definitely the structure responsible for falling in lust.

It is also vital to note and understand that the brain is the bridge between the physical and psychological (between the hardware and software). Certain psychological stimuli (memories, for example) can trigger a physical reaction, such as goosebumps. Conversely, physical stimulation (a specific smell, for example) can trigger an associated memory and/or emotional state. The specifics of this interrelationship can be daunting even to a professional, and so let it suffice for us to simply acknowledge here that the physical and psychological aspects of sex are linked by the brain.

Psychological Factors

First, let's look at how and why behavioral psychology and sexual psychology are linked. From an early age imagination stirs within us. We learn to visualize decisions leading to outcomes and to envision how pleasurable (rewarding) or painful (costly) those possible outcomes will be, both physically and psychologically. We even learn to enjoy the imagined pleasure. This speaks to why some become enthusiastic daydreamers.

This highly useful programming strategy becomes part of our thought and behavior patterns. Try visualizing this part of our psyche as a referee wearing a fortune teller's turban instead of a black cap. This little referee becomes a trusted guide in our process of thought/decision/behavior, and therefore, also becomes a part of our sexual identity when it develops.

With the help of our "ref," we learn the subtleties of social politics. We gain knowledge in the use of stereotypes and how they aid us with indexing information and recognizing patterns for quick decision making. We learn that being an outcast feels rotten while being accepted feels quite nice.

At some point (typically after we are stung by some ridicule, contempt, or other negative feedback) we learn to discriminate and be selective about the thoughts and ideas we share with others. We learn to keep a part of ourselves hidden in order to fit in. We learn to wear our mask and, because of these masks, the study of sexual psychology has suffered.

Sexual psychology has been approached by widely varying methods of study in recent history. Of the branches of scientific study dealing with human life, however, sexual psychology was born late and is still in its infancy. Biological and spiritual/supernatural/esoteric matters, for example, have received many times the attention; whether measured in scientific personnel, studies performed, or the actual results compiled.

The intricacies of sexual psychology, therefore, may be best thought of as fluid. When attempting to measure, quantify, or describe a fluid body (e.g., the water in a stream), rough estimates, grounded theories, and sound guesses are the best that can be hoped for.

The definition of "sexual deviance" is one of these problematic fluid calculations. The widely accepted definition of "sexual deviance" is as follows:

Sexual deviance is a culturally and historically specific concept referring to behaviors that involve individuals seeking erotic gratification through means that are considered odd, different, or unacceptable to either (a) most or (b) the most influential persons in one's community. Sexual deviance is commonly determined by the use of at least one of the following four criteria:

(1) The degree of consent by the parties involved
(2) The nature of the persons and objects involved in the behavior
(3) The action itself and the body parts involved
(4) The setting in which the behavior is performed

As societal norms shift, so do views on sexual behaviors. What was considered in Western culture to be normal and proper a century ago is considered utterly and ridiculously stifling by many today. Within a generation, the views of specific sexual behaviors change dramatically. Today, for example, all flavors of erotic and pornographic content are easily accessible and indexed for convenience. Thirty years ago, the societal imposition of propriety was so prevalent that it was a common practice (though risqué and not publicly discussed) to use catalogs containing undergarment ads as visual erotica, (i.e., using the images to enhance arousal during masturbation).

The moral implications of these increasingly rapid changes in societal norms are beyond the scope of this guide and each individual will, as always, weigh those issues based on their own value system. We will, therefore, proceed from here with the purpose of objective exploration in some psychological aspects of kink and BDSM.

The chief reason for focusing on sexual deviance and societal norms here is to help illustrate the stigma of being different. In most cultures, especially Western culture, there is a marked lack of openness and acceptance for ideas and behaviors that deviate from what the collective publicly deems as acceptable. This has undoubtedly affected, for the less rebellious individuals, the ability to freely and comfortably explore sexuality.

There have been momentous changes in how society regards kink and BDSM in recent years. For example:

(1)Many who have sought to explore kink and BDSM have found social networks such as the free site *fetlife.com*, where users can create a profile and communicate with thousands of "kinksters" around the globe. Each user has the ability to show as little or as much personal information as they choose.

(2)The qualifications for medical diagnosis of Sexual Sadism Disorder and Sexual Masochism Disorder (prevalent as a cover-all diagnosis and blatantly overused in the sexual psychology of recent decades) have been amended. Medical diagnosis now requires that there be evidence of a specific and clinically significant impairment to functioning in the individual's social life (i.e., professional, family, friend, intimate relationships, etc). Sadistic/masochistic behavior between two consenting adults no longer merits the clinical diagnosis without this new requirement.

(3)There has been a significant rise in scientific study of human sexuality and sexual psychology. Organizations like the Society for Scientific Study of Sexuality, websites such as The Science of BDSM (scienceofbdsm.blogspot.com), and writers like Jesse Bering (author of <u>Perv: The Sexual Deviant in All of Us</u>) are helping to liberate and illuminate that which has been kept hidden behind our masks; the "dirty" secrets of our most taboo sexual selves.

The commonly accepted ideas of what is "normal and acceptable" in society have a definite, daunting impact on the freedom of the curious individual to learn and explore. Many choose to suppress or deny any desires that risk disapproval or contempt. Recent developments in the acceptance and openness of the kink and BDSM community show, however, that the individual's views can also have an impact on the force of societal norm. This is happening in the same way a small dedicated team can build a manmade harbor that withstands the force of oceanic tides and currents. Stones are laid one at a time and, eventually, those stones form a cohesive unit that can defy a tidal force through the mutual advantage of its combined strength and solidarity.

The motivation for the individual to risk the contempt and ridicule of a peer group is, of course, the immense gratification to be felt when one is met with acceptance. Recent research even presents the possibility that practitioners of kink and BDSM may have a healthier self-image and a higher level of satisfaction and fulfillment in intimate relationships. When, through open and honest exploration, the individual learns to examine his or her own thoughts and behaviors with an open and scientific objectivity, then that individual may also turn this objective focus toward others in a supportive way. The openness within the growing BDSM/kink community makes this psychological gratification possible on three distinct levels:

1) The individual level (i.e., confidence, self-esteem).

2) The interpersonal/intimate level (i.e., acceptance, tolerance, and support of the exploration of intimate partner(s) with whom there are behavioral commonalities and shared interests).

3) The community level (acceptance, tolerance, and support of the exploration of acquaintances and strangers. *Note: This is not because of an intimate bond, but because the individual recognizes the importance of each seeking their own sexual identity and means of gratification*).

The level of frankness and openness involved in interpersonal exchange within the scope of kink/BDSM (e.g., sharing private thoughts, desires, and fantasies with another) implies not only courage and depth of character, but also an increased personal vulnerability, which necessitates a high level of trust. Strong relationships, regardless of conventional societal definitions, are formed.

In many kinky behaviors, intense emotional and psychological states may be actively sought and cultivated. To the vanilla observer, this may seem unhealthy, pointless, perverse, or even destructive. To those involved in this exploration of trust and desires, however, it can be rewarding, fulfilling, and empowering.

Individuals who remove their mask and earnestly investigate their sexual desires with another learn to share a powerful bond. It is a bond that can transcend convention and allow them to freely seek and share together. Practitioners may find obstacles and problems along the way, of course. That's part of life. Open and responsible exploration, however, is inherently superior to suppression and denial, especially with the added benefit of a supportive community that places such importance on safety.

BDSM / Kink Behaviors

Or wiitwd (What Is Is That We Do)

*Note: Every individual has a slightly different perception of roles and behaviors. Therefore, this will be a basic look at some broad examples. Individual practitioners and their specific behaviors seldom fit neatly into just one category. For more information on these behaviors, please see the Glossary section.

Most behaviors associated with the BDSM lifestyle fall into three categories:

Power Exchange- Participants either relinquish some degree of power/control ("submissive" or "bottom" role) or assume the power/control over another ("Dominant or Top role"). There are many subtle subcategories of power exchange, varying mostly in how the roles are named and the specifics of how and when the power exchange occurs. (e.g., Ageplay, Sadism/Masochism, Master/slave, etc.)

Polyamory- Participant(s) engage in erotic,

sexual, or intimate acts with more than one partner. There are, again, subcategories (e.g., Swingers, Cuckholds/Cuckqueans, etc.) depending on specifics of the parties involved and aspects of the interpersonal relations.

Fetishism- A fetish, by definition, is a nonsexual inanimate object that is given an erotic or sexual quality through association (e.g., high heels, stockings, garter belts, various other garments and objects). The term has also now come to encompass the spectrum of Paraphilias; a condition, in which, a person's sexual arousal and gratification depend on fantasizing about and/or engaging in sexual behavior that is atypical and extreme. Participants engage in acts centered around an array of objects, fantasies, behaviors and rituals.

"Kink" (defined as a "kink" or "bend" in sexuality, as opposed to "straight" or "vanilla") is a broader, more fluid term. Kink can encompass all the aforementioned BDSM behaviors, as well as anything deemed outside the social norms of any specific place and time. It could be asserted that this includes any sexual orientation or gender identity other than strictly heterosexual or "straight".

Sexual Identity Spectrum

For most of Western culture, the terms "gender" and "sex" are used interchangeably and thus, incorrectly. Due to long standing stereotypes and a widespread distaste for any condition beyond "normal", the specifics of the Sexual Identity Spectrum are seldom considered by anyone other than the individual exploring his or her own deviations from the societal norm. This social stigma and the commonplace reluctance to dismiss it have limited access and education concerning the Sexual Identity Spectrum, which this guide will now address.

The greatest misconception to address here is that biological sex and not gender are the same thing. Gender is not inherently connected to one's physical anatomy.

Biological Gender (sex) includes physical attributes such as external genitalia, sex chromosomes, gonads, sex hormones, and internal reproductive structures. At birth, these factors are used to assign sex; that is, to identify an individual as male or female.

Gender is a far more intricate and accurate way to describe a person's sexuality. Gender is the complex interrelationship between an individual's biological sex , gender identity or internal sense of self (i.e., male, female, both or neither), and outward presentations and behaviors (i.e., gender expression). Together, these three values combine to form an authentic sense of gender, both in how individuals experience and project their own gender as well as how others perceive it.

These three values can be independently characterized across a wide range of possibilities. Instead of the binary model for a strictly biological understanding of gender, a far richer tapestry of biology, gender expression, and gender identity intersect in a multidimensional array of possibilities. The Sexual Identity Spectrum undeniably represents a more authentic model of human gender.

Anonymous "Kinkster" Surveys

Name: Bill
Age: 24
Gender Identity: Male
Preferred Role(s): Daddy Dominant
Level of involvement in BDSM/kink lifestyle:
Part-time, I would want to have times set aside for it.
I'm generally more discreet.
Me and R--- are working towards real life, right now it's only online.
How long have you been actively involved in BDSM/kink lifestyle?
Eight months.
List some of your favorite kinks/fetishes/fantasies.
Daddy Dom/little girl role play.
What do you identify as the single, most rewarding experience you've had in your exploration and/or practice of BDSM/kink?
Just when I realized that the way I've always wanted to treat a girl...Is already a fetish...It kinda blew my mind and just made me feel....Found. I can't think of a better way to describe it. When I told her all the rules that I'd like to use and they made her just so excited, it just made me feel complete. That was a pretty positive moment for me.

What do you identify as the most discouraging, negative experience you've had in your exploration and/or practice of BDSM/kink?

Me taking things too far and hurting her unintentionally. Not physically, but emotionally. That's always the worst part to any relationship. Getting so caught up in my own head that I forget I have a Little to think about. The worst experience I've had is when things got to the point that we couldn't do it. We both got so worked up that we had to shut it down. That was the hardest thing about our experimentation so far.

What has been your primary source of information and knowledge concerning the BDSM/kink lifestyle?

The Internet.

How do you believe that BDSM/kink can personally enrich a life?

It can add something fresh and different. It can remove the person from the stresses of their normal life. It's definitely a good way to unwind.

Name: Caitlin
Age: 20
Gender Identity: Female
Preferred Role(s): Submissive, Little, Baby girl
Level of involvement in BDSM/kink lifestyle:
Part-time. Secret from my family. Online, for now.
How long have you been actively involved in BDSM/kink lifestyle?
Two years.
List some of your favorite kinks/fetishes/fantasies.
Daddy Dom/little girl role play, Puppy play, Bondage, Spankings, and Public play.
What do you identify as the single, most rewarding experience you've had in your exploration and/or practice of BDSM/kink?
I remember the first time Daddy told me I was a good girl. I felt so incredibly happy and relieved to just hear those words from him. I felt like I was really in tune with his wants and needs as a Daddy and that's the best feeling I've ever had. I mean, every time he tells me I'm a good girl I get so happy.
What do you identify as the most discouraging, negative experience you've had in your exploration and/or practice of BDSM/kink?
Being told I needed to try harder in the bedroom in a previous relationship. It kinda

hit a nerve and I didn't like it very much. He made me feel really insecure and insignificant, like I wasn't good enough.

What has been your primary source of information and knowledge concerning the BDSM/kink lifestyle?

Networking online, with friends, and group chats.

How do you believe that BDSM/kink can personally enrich a life?

I definitely think it's a good experience to have in life. I didn't know I'd love it as much as I do. It's definitely something that releases stress pretty easily for me. It helps you get comfortable with who you really are. You could be someone who is a submissive or a Dominant and you don't even know it. It opens up your mind to so many different things and possibilities.

Name: Emmanuelle
Age: 52
Gender Identity: Female
Preferred Role(s): Submissive
Level of involvement in BDSM/kink lifestyle:
Part-time, as much as work allows. Open with my daughters and kinky friends, but secret for the most part. In real time. I'm married to my Dominant.
How long have you been actively involved in BDSM/kink lifestyle?
Two months.
List some of your favorite kinks/fetishes/fantasies.
Spanking, D/s, roleplaying, rough play
What do you identify as the single, most rewarding experience you've had in your exploration and/or practice of BDSM/kink?
Learning and experimenting with edging. Surrendering the burden of physical pleasure to my Dominant and having my orgasm controlled and so long denied is a very new and gratifying experience. It has yielded the best orgasm of my life, to date. I am eagerly anticipating the next.
What do you identify as the most discouraging, negative experience you've had in your exploration and/or practice of BDSM/kink?
Butt plugs! My husband/Dom and I tried and we're just not having success with it. I

really want to enjoy this and I know it would please my Dom, but I have anxiety concerning hygiene and it's difficult to overcome. The difficulty overcoming personal anxiety about something I want to experience and enjoy is discouraging.

What has been your primary source of information and knowledge concerning the BDSM/kink lifestyle?

Books and my daughter who is also actively involved in a BDSM lifestyle.

How do you believe that BDSM/kink can personally enrich a life?

It makes you more self-aware and more confident which flows over in to the rest of your life. Your eyes are also more open to the beauty of the human body in all its forms.

Name: Hector

Age: 54

Gender Identity: Male

Preferred Role(s): Dominant

Level of involvement in BDSM/kink lifestyle:

Part-time, for the moment. Open with my wife and a few friends, but mostly secret. In real time. I'm married to my submissive.

How long have you been actively involved in BDSM/kink lifestyle?

 Two months.

List some of your favorite kinks/fetishes/fantasies.

Spanking, threesomes, renaissance roleplaying, rough play

What do you identify as the single, most rewarding experience you've had in your exploration and/or practice of BDSM/kink?

The openness between me and my sub. Our communication has vastly improved and increased. We now know more about each other than we ever have before. All of a sudden we're talking more and more honestly.

What do you identify as the most discouraging, negative experience you've had in your exploration and/or practice of BDSM/kink?

I'm really new, so having to take it all at a slow pace is frustrating at times. When you first learn about it you want to jump in with both feet, but there's a lot to take in and you've got to take it slowly or it will overwhelm you, especially your emotions.

What has been your primary source of information and knowledge concerning BDSM/kink lifestyle?

Fetlife.com and books

How do you believe that BDSM/kink can personally enrich a life?

You can confront your fears and handle much stronger emotions that most people would just fall away from.

Name: Darlene
Age: 19
Gender Identity: Female
Preferred Role(s): Submissive
Level of involvement in BDSM/kink lifestyle:
Part-time. Open with some, secret with most. Mostly online.
How long have you been actively involved in BDSM/kink lifestyle?
Five months.
List some of your favorite kinks/fetishes/fantasies.
Rape fantasy, incest fantasy, daddy-little girl curiosity, I love being choked and spanked.
What do you identify as the single, most rewarding experience you've had in your exploration and/or practice of BDSM/kink?
When I first explored BDSM it was light, I was tied with a tie around my wrists and ankles and spanked with a belt on my back and with a hand on my ass, I absolutely loved it. I wish the knot held and restrained me better, though.
What do you identify as the most discouraging, negative experience you've had in your exploration and/or practice of BDSM/kink?
Worst experience was when I had to imagine my younger sister getting fucked and I had to watch, direct and possibly partake.
What has been your primary source of

information and knowledge concerning BDSM/kink lifestyle?

My primary source has been my "training" with a couple, reading and social networks

How do you believe that BDSM/kink can personally enrich a life?

It can enrich a person's life by letting them release a part of themselves that is hidden in their every day life, it lets them become open about their vulnerabilities and increases their self esteem. It also allows them to become more comfortable with their sexuality.

Name: Janice
Age: 19
Gender Identity: Female
Preferred Role(s): Babygirl, Submissive
Level of involvement in BDSM/kink lifestyle:
Part-time. Open.
How long have you been actively involved in BDSM/kink lifestyle?
A few months.
List some of your favorite kinks/fetishes/fantasies.
Rape fantasy, incest fantasy, DDLG, ABDL.
What do you identify as the single, most rewarding experience you've had in your exploration and/or practice of BDSM/kink?
Best experience was going out with my Dom and "siblings" in public and being open with everyone.
What do you identify as the most discouraging, negative experience you've had in your exploration and/or practice of BDSM/kink?
Worst experience was when my Dom went too hard and made me feel worthless.
What has been your primary source of information and knowledge concerning BDSM/kink lifestyle?
Social network, Fetlife.
How do you believe that BDSM/kink can personally enrich a life?
For me bdsm makes me more open to myself

and everyone around me and definitely increases my self esteem.

Name: Emily

Age: 27

Gender Identity: Female

Preferred Role(s): slave

Level of involvement in BDSM/kink lifestyle:

Full time, as much as I can manage. I am open with friends and family, though professionally I am discreet. I am primarily an online slave with aspirations to move into a real time dynamic.

How long have you been actively involved in BDSM/kink lifestyle?

Two years

List some of your favorite kinks/fetishes/fantasies.

Total power exchange relationships, physical masochism, incest roleplay, domestic discipline, and rape fantasy

What do you identify as the single, most rewarding experience you've had in your exploration and/or practice of BDSM/kink?

The most personally edifying and rewarding experience, for me, has been the transition from submissive to slave, which for many people can mean many different things. For me it means submitting every aspect of my life to the authority of my Owner/Dominant, including surrendering the power to end our relationship. He doesn't micromanage my life. For the most part, I run my own life with a few exceptions. What it really means is that he can step in at any point and change anything he wants without warning or explanation. What is required of me is unhesitating obedience and unfaltering loyalty to him and to our dynamic.

This has been incredibly edifying because 1) My Owner is a mindful and conscientious Dominant. He takes great pains to train and guide me in ways that help me to grow as a person and expand self-awareness. 2) Serving as a slave, with high standards concerning obedience, has taught me so much about my capabilities and deepened my understanding of loyalty, integrity, and attachment within the context of relationships.

What do you identify as the most discouraging, negative experience you've had in your exploration and/or practice of BDSM/kink?

It is difficult to pin down a truly negative experience because even the disheartening incidents have proven edifying. The most taxing experience has been the realization that my role as slave does not and will not include emotional attachment or partnership in any sense with my Owner. Reconciling my role as a slave with my desires as a woman and emotional needs as a person has left a gap that is psychologically stressful and emotionally painful. It's a struggle that I tackle daily that does not fade and does not make me stronger. It leaves me raw and weak, but learning to live with the daily pain and vulnerability has increased my understanding of slavery and my desire to be a slave.

What has been your primary source of information and knowledge concerning BDSM/kink lifestyle?

I've gleaned the bulk of my information from non-fiction books on the subject of BDSM.

How do you believe that BDSM/kink can personally enrich a life?

I find that many adults are not fully, sexually self-aware. Ignoring this portion of your life is just as detrimental as ignoring other biological needs such as nutrition, sleep, and exercise. Self-awareness is probably the most effective tool anyone can use to navigate their own life. Exploration of the kink lifestyle, when done properly and safely, can yield considerable self-discovery. This adds to your sexual, psychological, and emotional health, yielding a well-balanced, healthy lifestyle.

Name: Jennifer
Age: 44
Gender Identity: Female
Preferred Role(s): Top
Level of involvement in BDSM/kink lifestyle:
Part time. Partially open and partially secret. Real time.
How long have you been actively involved in BDSM/kink lifestyle?
Five years.
List some of your favorite kinks/fetishes/fantasies.
D/s, choking, and MMF.
What do you identify as the single, most rewarding experience you've had in your exploration and/or practice of BDSM/kink?
Finding myself.
What do you identify as the most discouraging, negative experience you've had in your exploration and/or practice of BDSM/kink?
The drama in the lifestyle.
What has been your primary source of information and knowledge concerning BDSM/kink lifestyle?
Social networking.
How do you believe that BDSM/kink can personally enrich a life?
Can deepen your understanding of yourself. It can bring happiness.

Glossary

*Note: This glossary is intended to be a practical reference for the novice practitioner or the beginning researcher. For this reason, there are many terms and definitions not covered here. There are dozens of new terms, associations, variations and subsets of slang that emerge continually.

24/7 – A constant. 24 hours a day, 7 days a week. At all times.

A

Ablutophilia – Attraction to or tendency toward sexual arousal/behavior/fantasies involving baths or showers.

Abrasion - (See also: Cutting , Knife Play) Literally meaning a wearing, grinding, or rubbing away by friction. In BDSM play this may involve stimulating the surface of the body with abrasive materials such as rough silk, leather, sandpaper, brushes, etc.

Acomoclitic - Attraction to or tendency toward sexual arousal/behavior/fantasies involving hairless genitals (see gynelophilous, hirsutophilia, hyphephilia, pubephilia, trichophilia).

Acrophilia - Attraction to or tendency toward

sexual arousal/behavior/fantasies involving high places.

Acrotomophilia - Attraction to or tendency toward sexual arousal/behavior/fantasies involving an amputee partner.

Acousticophilia - Attraction to or tendency toward sexual arousal/behavior/fantasies involving sounds.

Actirasty - Attraction to or tendency toward sexual arousal/behavior/fantasies involving exposure to the sun's rays.

Acucullophilia – Attraction to or tendency toward sexual arousal/behavior/fantasies involving men who are circumcised.

Adult Toy Chest – A place where one keeps their sex toys. A sex toy box.

Aftercare – Period of rest and discussion after a session or scene of play.

Agalmatophilia/Pygmalionism - Attraction to or tendency toward sexual arousal/behavior/fantasies involving statues/mannequins or immobility.

Age Play – play that involves assuming the role of someone of a different age. Most commonly, one of the adults takes on the younger role, usually in the submissive capacity.

Agonophilia - Attraction to or tendency toward sexual arousal/behavior/fantasies involving pseudo-rape, pretend struggle or wrestling play.

Agoraphilia - Attraction to or tendency toward sexual arousal/behavior/fantasies involving sex in public places.

Agrexophilia - Attraction to or tendency toward sexual arousal/behavior/fantasies involving having others aware of one's sexual activities.

Algolagnia/Algalagnia - Attraction to or tendency toward sexual arousal/behavior/fantasies generally involving pain.

Algophilia – Attraction to or tendency toward sexual arousal/behavior/fantasies involving the firsthand experience of pain.

Alligator Clamp – A type of nipple clamp with tips that have teeth resembling an alligators mouth. Most clamps of this style come with removable rubber tips and have adjustment screws to limit how far they can close.

Allorgasmia - Attraction to or tendency toward sexual arousal/behavior/fantasies involving fantasizing about someone other than one's partner.

Allotriorasty - Attraction to or tendency toward sexual arousal/behavior/fantasies involving intimate partners of other nationalities or races.

Alphmegamia - Attraction to or tendency toward sexual arousal/behavior/fantasies involving older men.

Altocalciphilia - Attraction to or tendency toward sexual arousal/behavior/fantasies involving high heels (see retifism).

Alt-sex – Abbreviation for alternative sexuality, encompassing BDSM/kink/fetish, polyamory, swing, and other "non-mainstream" forms of erotic interest and expression.

Alvinolagnia - Attraction to or tendency toward sexual arousal/behavior/fantasies involving the stomach/belly/abdomen (see partialism).

Amaurophilia - Attraction to or tendency toward sexual arousal/behavior/fantasies involving a partner who is unable to see during sex; a blind/blindfolded sex partner.

Anal Beads - A set of strung beads designed and used to insert into the anus.

Anaclitism - Attraction to or tendency toward sexual arousal/behavior/fantasies involving activities or objects one was exposed to as an infant.

Anal Dildo – A dildo that is intended to be used with the anus as the receptor.

Anal Intercourse – Sex using the anus as the receptor.

Anal Play - This is generally play where the anus may be penetrated with either beads, ice, dildos, anal plugs, penis, or fist. Rimming the anus with a finger or toys stimulates the nerves which can create a more intense orgasm. Stimulating the male's prostrate gland (males) can cause increased intensity of orgasm.

Anal Plug - (See also: Dildo , Vibrator) A specially designed dildo for use in the anus that is shaped in a way so that it will not "fall out". Most commonly inserted and left in the anus for a given amount of time.

Anal Sex - (See also: Rimming) Any sexual activity involving the anus. Examples are; rimming (oral), Butt / Anal Plugs, Dildos, and penile penetration.

Anasteemaphilia - Attraction to or tendency toward sexual arousal/behavior/fantasies involving substantially taller or shorter partners.

Androidism - Attraction to or tendency toward sexual arousal/behavior/fantasies involving robots with human features.

Ankle Cuffs – Attachable cuffs, generally made of leather, used to restrain and/or immobilize a submissive's legs.

Ankle Restraint – Any device including ankle cuffs that immobilizes a submissive's legs.

Animal Play – Role-play where one or more partners assume the identity of an animal. Furries are considered a subset of this group and often dress in elaborate animal costumes. Animal play involves humans only, and should not in any way be confused with bestiality or zoophilia.

Animal Training – Training where the Dominant has his submissive play the part of an animal, such as a horse or a kitten. The most common is "puppy play".

Anophelorastia - Attraction to or tendency toward sexual arousal/behavior/fantasies involving defiling or ravaging a partner.

Antholagnia - Attraction to or tendency toward sexual arousal/behavior/fantasies involving floral scents.

Aphephilia - Attraction to or tendency toward sexual arousal/behavior/fantasies involving being touched.

Apotemnophilia - Attraction to or tendency toward sexual arousal/behavior/fantasies involving self-amputation or the idea of performing self-amputation.

Arachnephilia - Attraction to or tendency toward sexual arousal/behavior/fantasies involving spiders.

Archetype – Jungian term for symbolic role which represents an aspect of the human psyche. BDSM role-play often draws on archetypes in creating role personae.

Asexual – A person who has no sexual feelings or desires.

Asphyxiaphilia – Attraction to or tendency toward sexual arousal/behavior/fantasies involving breath control, asphyxiation, or choking.

Asphyxiation - (See also Breath Control , Choking) Commonly referred to as "breath control". Refers to play involving control of or restriction of air and / or oxygen to the brain. Any form of stopping, controlling or impeding breathing freely including choking, smothering and hoods with tubes, sacks, plastics, etc, is asphyxia. Sometimes used to cause a more intense orgasm.

Asthenolagnia - Attraction to or tendency toward sexual arousal/behavior/fantasies involving weakness and/or being humiliated.

Auctioned for Charity - (See also: Competitions) Involves play where the partner (usually the submissive) is auctioned off to others for charitable purposes.

Autoclave – Professional sterilization device for piercing equipment.

Auto-erotic Asphyxiation – The erotic practice of asphyxiation (breath control, choking) on oneself.

Autagonistophilia - Attraction to or tendency toward sexual arousal/behavior/fantasies involving exhibiting one's naked body or genitals to strangers while on stage, while being photographed.

Autogynephilia – Attraction to or tendency toward sexual arousal/behavior/fantasies involving cross-dressing.

B

Ball Gag – A device with a rubber ball and straps, which secures the ball in the bottom's mouth.

Ball Stretching - Play which involves stretching the testicles and scrotum.

Ball Torture – Causing pain to the male testicles, also included in CBT or cock and ball torture.

Ball Toys – Toys used for playing with the scrotum – such as weights, straps, etc.

Ball Weights – Weights used to stretch the scrotum. See Ball Stretching.

Ballet Boots – Extremely high heeled boots that require you to stand on the ends of your toes rather than the sole of your foot. Sometimes also referred to as bondage boots.

Barbell – A straight piece of metal used in piercing, as opposed to a ring.

Bathroom Use Control - (See also: Catheterization , Enemas) Scenes where the Dominant restricts or takes control over the submissive's bodily functions.

BDSM – Acronym combining B&D (bondage & discipline), D/s (dominance & submission) and S/M (sadomasochism). A continuum of erotic practice and expression involving the consensual use of restraint, intense sensory stimulation, power exchange and fantasy role-play.

BDSM Toy Box (or Toy Box) - A place where one keeps their BDSM gear or play equipment.

Beating - (See also: Spanking , Caning) Striking the body with various objects or the hand.

Being Serviced - Play dependent upon and resulting from the Dominant instructing the submissive on exactly how He / She wants the submissive to perform.

Belonephilia - Attraction to or tendency toward sexual arousal/behavior/fantasies involving pins, needles, or other sharp objects

Bestiality - Incorporation of the use of animals for sexual pleasure. Not to be confused with animal role playing. This form of play can be very dangerous.

Biastophilia - Attraction to or tendency toward sexual arousal/behavior/fantasies involving the violent rape of a victim.

Bisexual – state of being in which an individual is attracted to (or has the potential to be attracted to) people of more than one gender.

Biting - Scenes involving the biting of the skin to induce pain.

BJ – expression for blowjob (fellatio).

Blindfold - An object used to block a person's sense of sight. Also erotic behavior which involves temporarily blocking the sense of sight.

Blood sports (Blood Play) - A range of techniques in which the submissive's skin is broken and blood is allowed to escape. Such as cutting, using needles, etc.

Blowjob – Fellatio, head, the act of oral sex performed on the penis.

Body Art – Artful body modification including: piercing, tattoos and brandings.

Body Modification – Making alterations to the appearance of the body. Includes, but is not limited to, tattoos, piercings, brandings, scarification.

Bondage - (Bondage and Discipline) Practice of using physical restraint and/or confinement to produce or enhance erotic arousal.

Boot Worship - The practice of play involving a fetish for boots / shoes.

Bottom - Person who receives sensation and/or consents to be restrained or controlled during play; sometimes used interchangeably with the term submissive.

Boy – Term for male submissive (also spelled "boi").

Boy Toy – A male who is submissive to a Dominant.

Branding - (See also: Cutting , Knife Play , Tattoo, Body Modification, Body Art) Making a permanent or semi-permanent scar on the skin, usually by burning it with a hot metal object, as practiced on livestock.

Brat – Term for a sub who has a tendency to (intentionally or unintentionally) get the attention of a Dominant by "acting up."

Breast / Chest Bondage - The restriction /

bondage of the breast /chest area for erotic reasons using various types of fastenings (i.e., rope, scarves, etc.).

Breast Whipping - Whipping of the submissive's chest area using a variety of items which include: floggers, whips, cat tails, paddles, etc.

Breath Control - another type of "edgeplay" whereby the submissive's breath is stopped for a short period of time to increase pleasurable sensations. Also called asphyxiaphilia, autoerotic asphyxiation, breath games, breathplay and hypoxyphilia.

Brown Showers (Scat) - The practice of play involving feces.

Bruising – Subdural hematoma: tissue damage results in blood being trapped under the skin. A condition which may occur as a result of various types of impact play.

Bukake- Sexual scene where many men masturbate on and give a "semen bath" to a willing submissive.

Bullwhip – A long, heavy leather whip usually longer than 4 feet.

Butterfly Board – A wooden board which a male's scrotum can be nailed or pinned onto.

Buttplug – a "sextoy" shaped to fit into and stay inside the rectum.

Buttplug Harness – Usually a leather harness that prevents a buttplug from being removed either intentional or accidentally from the rectum.

C

Cage – (Caging, Caged, To cage) A bondage practice, wherein the submissive is kept inside a cage. They can be so small as to restrict motion or large enough for two or more people.

Cages - Most common is the use of a large animal cage. Construction of a cage can be of wood, steel, fencing material. Used to confine the submissive, for play or punishment.

Candle – A source of hot wax, which is dripped onto the bottom's body in BDSM play.

Cane – A slender rod used for impact play; traditionally made of rattan, but there are now canes made of various materials.

Caning - (See also: Beating , Whipping) Striking or whipping of the body with a cane, usually made of bamboo, rattan, or various other materials.

Cat – An expression for a BDSM tool of discipline – the "cat o' nine tails".

Cat O' Nine Tails – a whip that has exactly 9 strands. Some have a knot at the end for increased sensation or sting.

Catheter – Flexible tube used in medicine. (See also: Urethral Catheter)

Catheterization - (See also: Bathroom Use Control , Enemas , Urethral Play) A medical procedure involving the iInsertion of a flexible tube into an orifice, commonly the urethra.

Cathterophilia – Attraction to or tendency toward sexual arousal/behavior/fantasies involving the use or insertion of catheters.

Cattle Prod - An electrical prodding device used to herd animals, more frequently for cattle.

CBT – Cock and Ball Torture – Causing pain to the male genital area; usually in controlled, consensual BDSM scenes.

Cells or Closets – (see also: cage) Small spaces used in play or scenes which involve confinement.

Chains – Metal links; used to immobilize or restrict the movement of a submissive's body.

Chastity Belt - (See also: Enforced Chastity) A device (usually lockable) which when worn prevents any type of genital stimulation.

Chezolagnia – masturbating while defecating.

Choking - (See also: Asphyxiation , Breath Control) Compression of the esophagus and/or carotid arteries in order to restrict air or blood flow to the brain.

Choreophilia - Attraction to or tendency toward sexual arousal/behavior/fantasies involving dancing to the point of orgasmic release.

Chores (Domestic Service) - (See also: Housework) Scenes where the Dominant requires the submissive to perform chores and / or domestic service. May involve sexually pleasing clothing (i.e., maid outfits) or nudity.

Chrematistophilia - Attraction to or tendency toward sexual arousal/behavior/fantasies involving having to pay for sex or being the victim of a theft perpetrated by a sex partner.

Chrysophilia - Attraction to or tendency toward sexual arousal/behavior/fantasies involving gold or gold colored objects (see Timophilia).

Circumcision – The cutting away of some or the entire foreskin, in males. In the female, circumcision usually refers to the removal of the clitoral hood.

Clamp – Generic term for any BDSM toy (even if garnered at a hardware store) that can clamp some body part of a submissive.

Claustrophilia - Attraction to or tendency toward sexual arousal/behavior/fantasies involving being confined in a small space

Clingfilm – Generic term for plastic wrap which is used in mummification scenes.

Clip – Generic term for any BDSM toy (even if garnered at a hardware store) that can clip some body part of a submissive.

Clitoridectomy – Surgical removal of the clitoris.

Clitorilingus – Tonguing the clitoris.

Clothespins – wooden or plastic clothespins, typically used to produce pain sensation on the skin. Commonly used on nipples and genital areas.

Clover Nipple Clamps – Type of adjustable nipple clamps that tightens as it is pulled. Also known as Japanese Clover Nipple Clamps.

Cock & Ball Torture (CBT) - any form of restraint or painful treatment to a male's genitals.

Cock Cage – a CBT device that is intended to encase a penis shaft inside it. Can be either a solid or web design.

Cock Cuff - a chastity device that consists of a tube welded to a handcuff, usually both made of stainless steel. The tube houses the penis and the handcuff closes snugly at the base of the scrotum, making removal all but impossible without unlocking the handcuff. A very effective chastity device.

Cock Ring - Rubber, metal, or leather type ring used to strap around the base of the cock and balls to enhance erection.

Cock Strap – Leather or neoprene strap that wraps around the base of cock and balls to enhance erection.

Cock Sucking – see "fellatio".

Cock Torture – Cock and ball torture without the ball torture. Administering or directing pain only to the penis shaft.

Cock Worship - (See also: Homage , Licking)
Play which involves the fantasy of worshiping
the cock. Performed mostly by the submissive
to the Dominant.

Collar - A collar worn around the neck of the
submissive/slave/bottom to indicate status
of commitment, submissiveness or
ownership. These can be made of leather,
steel, rubber, rope, or various other
materials.

Collar and Leash – Worn by the bottom
during this type of BDSM play. The Dominant
holds the leash and the bottom must follow
and obey. Collars are also worn by the
submissive as symbols of commitment,
submissiveness and ownership.

Collaring Ceremony – Ritual whereby a
dominant and a submissive commit to a
relationship or agreement, often assuming
the roles of Master/Mistress and slave
respectively. Along with the slave receiving a
collar as a symbol, the parties may also sign
a contract spelling out the specific terms of
the relationship.

Competitions (With Other Subs) - (See also:
Auctioned for Charity) Scenes involving
competitive-type sports or play with other

submissives.

Condom – Latex "rubber" sheath that goes over the penis to prevent the exchange of bodily fluids during intercourse. Also known as a rain coat, gym cap, shower cap, Jimmy hat, hot rod gasket, love glove, muffler, cock sock, goalie, or hazmat suit.

Consent – To give approval. The BDSM code of "safe, sane and consensual" or "SSC" is the cornerstone of BDSM play, with consent being the most important.

Contract – A written agreement between partners outlining the extent of their relationship. These contracts may not have the capacity to be legally enforced, but they are often used to define the relationship for the benefit of the parties involved.

Coprolagnia – Sexual excitement derived from eating feces.

Coprolalia - Attraction to or tendency toward sexual arousal/behavior/fantasies involving obscene language or writing

Corporal Punishment – The act of administering pain to another with the purpose of punishment. Commonly used as a method to alter undesired behavior patterns, but may also be purely an act of retribution.

Corset – Very popular clothing item that cinches and narrows the waist and gives the female an "hourglass" figure.

Coulrophilia - Attraction to or tendency toward sexual arousal/behavior/fantasies involving clowns.

Crop – A type of whip used in horseback riding, quite popular in BDSM scenes.

Cross – see St. Andrew's Cross.

Cross Dressing – Dressing in clothing worn by the opposite sex.

Crotch Torture - Any form of torture to the male or female genital area.

Crucifixion – BDSM play wherein a submissive is tied to a cross.

Crurophilia - Attraction to or tendency toward sexual arousal/behavior/fantasies involving legs.

Crush fetishism - Attraction to or tendency toward sexual arousal/behavior/fantasies involving seeing small creatures being crushed.

Cuffs - A leather or metal bondage device

used to restrict movement. Usually locks around the limbs in order to place the submissive in a precarious position.

Cunnilingus – The act of oral sex performed on the vagina.

Cunt Torture – Stimulation or pain inflicted on the female genitals.

Cupping – The placing of suction devices on the skin to increase blood flow. Typically these are used on the nipples and the genitalia. Increasing the blood flow increase sensation as well.

Cutting – Cutting the submissive's skin with a sterile knife. These can be either temporary or permanent. Made permanent by putting a sterile foreign substances into them before they heal. NOT for beginners.

Cutting - (See also: Abrasion , Branding ,Knife Play, Blood Play) Cutting the surface of the skin with sharp objects, generally for the thrill, sensation, or to create scars or marks.

D

D/s – Popular abbreviation for Dominance and submission. A power exchange relationship between a Top and bottom where one is Dominant (recieves control or power) and the other submissive (relinquishes control or power). Can be for a scene or a long-term relationship or anything in between.

Dacryphilia - Attraction to or tendency toward sexual arousal/behavior/fantasies involving witnessing an intimate partner crying.

Daddy (Daddy Dom)- A role taken on by some dominants; especially common in age play.

Dendrophilia - Attraction to or tendency toward sexual arousal/behavior/fantasies involving trees.

Depilation – Removal of hair.

Diapers – Waterproof or absorbent garment worn in BDSM play for the object of child-playing scenes.

Dilation - The term used when a woman's cervix is dilated (opened) to aid in childbirth. In BDSM play dilation occurs when a speculum (pelvic exam device) is used to open the cervix for medical scening.

Dildo - (See also: Anal Plug , Vibrator) From the French term meaning "I please myself). A manufactured phallic-shaped device designed and intended for insertion into the body. Early versions were made of stuffed animal gut, leather, or ceramics. Today they are most commonly crafted of molded latex.

Discipline – May include a wide range of acts such as whipping, spanking, immobilization/confinement, verbal orders, etc, generally for the purpose of training a submissive.

Dittle Sound – (see Sounding, Urethral Sound) A straight urethral sound.

DM – Acronym for Dungeon Monitor. In a BDSM play party, this is the person who is to watch the scene(s) to ensure house rules are followed and the play is safe.

Dog-Training – Role-play games involving treating the bottom as a dog. Similar to Pony Training where the bottom is treated like a pony.

Dom – Short for Dominant.

Dominance & Submission (D&S, D/s) – Consensual empowerment of one person by another to enhance or produce erotic arousal. Sometimes referred to as "erotic power exchange."

Dominant (Dom) – In a power exchange

relationship, a Dominant is the person entrusted with power and/or control by a submissive.

Dominant Masochist – A bottom who enjoys directing a top to deliver erotic pain or other intense sensation. See also submissive sadist, topping from the bottom.

Domination – Taking the Dominant role – controlling the behavior of the bottom or submissive.

Domme – A female Dominant.

Doraphilia - Attraction to or tendency toward sexual arousal/behavior/fantasies involving skin, animal fur, or leather (see Hyphephilia).

Double Penetration – Simultaneous penetration by two objects.

Double Penetration - Play involving the penetration of two objects into bodily orifices (penetration of the mouth / rectum / vagina, etc.)

Douche, Douching – Injecting of a liquid, usually water, into the anus or vagina, usually for hygiene purposes prior to sex or play.

DP – Abbreviation for Double Penetration.

Dracophilia - Attraction to or tendency toward sexual arousal/behavior/fantasies involving dragons, serpents, or similar creatures.

Dungeon – A room arranged for BDSM play, often with special equipment or furniture, sometimes with thematic decoration.

Dysmorphophilia - Attraction to or tendency toward sexual arousal/behavior/fantasies involving deformed or physically impaired partners (see Teratophilia).

E

Ecdyosis – Sexual arousal from stripping in front of an audience

Ecdysiast – One who finds pleasure in the act of stripping in front of an audience.

Ecouteurism - Attraction to or tendency toward sexual arousal/behavior/fantasies involving listening (without permission) to others having sex.

Edgeplay – Technically, this refers to knife play. But it has come to mean anything "on the edge." Or considered "Extreme" It can even include fisting, asphyxia, play piercings, needle play, etc. One person's edge can be another's norm so there are no hard and fast rules defining what "edgeplay" is.

Edgeplayer – A person who partakes in edgeplay.

Electrical Play – Using electricity for stimulation. Professionally made electrical units are used – like the "tens" unit and the "violet wand."

Electricity - (See also: TENS Unit , Violet Wand) In BDSM play, a safely regulated electrical charge is sometimes used to stimulate various body parts. Popular devices include "TENS" units designed for the relief of muscle and back pain; and "Violet Wands" which use a radio frequency discharge.

Electrolysis – Permanent hair removal that involves a specialized electrical device.

Electrophilia - Attraction to or tendency toward sexual arousal/behavior/fantasies involving electricity.

Electrotorture -Another, more dramatic, term for electrical play.

Emasculation – Traditionally, this is the permanent removal of the male sex organs. Sometimes simulated or symbolized through the use of a chastity device or through imposed (via power exchange) restrictions forbidding typical male behavior such a urinating while standing.

EMS Unit – see Tens Unit.

Endorphin – A chemical produced in the body that seems to be involved in regulating the perception of pain. Endorphins give a "rush" similar to adrenaline and it is speculated that their release is the cause of the phenomenon known as "subspace."

Endorphin High (Endorphin Rush) – Alternate name for sub-space or bottom-space, generally induced by intense stimulation; endorphins are regulated by the central nervous system in response to such stimuli, especially pain.

Endytophilia - Attraction to or tendency toward sexual arousal/behavior/fantasies involving partners who are clothed.

Enema – A thorough anal douche using a bag and tube.

Enema Play – Using the enema as a BDSM device in play.

Enforced Chastity – Chastity play where the Dom controls a sub's sexual frequency and ability to experience genital stimulation or sexual pleasure, usually with a chastity belt or other chastity device.

Erotic Pain – Sensation which may be painful, but is enjoyable in an erotic context.

Erotic Power Exchange (Power Exchange) (EPE) – Alternate term for Dominance & submission (see above).

Erotographomania - Attraction to or tendency toward sexual arousal/behavior/fantasies involving writing love poems or letters.

Erotophonophilia - Attraction to or tendency toward sexual arousal/behavior/fantasies involving lust related murder.

Examinations - Scenes involving some type of physical examination (i.e. medical exams). May include the use of medical (or similar) equipment.

Exercise - Play which involves forcing one's submissive to exercise as a form of control / humiliation (may include lifting, running, weight-lifting, etc.).

Exhibitionism - Attraction to or tendency toward sexual arousal/behavior/fantasies involving showing one's body (commonly genitals) in public.

Extreme Restraints – A Bondage device that is very strict or unusually confining.

Eye Contact Restrictions – Restrictions (generally imposed upon the bottom/submissive) against any eye contact with the Dominant (i.e., forcing submissive to look away / look down).

F

Face Fucking – Another term for fellatio; a blowjob.

Face Slapping - Involves play where a moderate amount of slapping of the face is used for humiliation / control.

Fainting – A temporary loss of consciousness, usually caused by lack of oxygen to the brain.

Fantasy Abandonment - Play which involves the fantasy of abandonment. Possibly leaving the submissive in a deserted area or public area for a short period of time.

Fantasy Rape - Scenes where the Dominant fulfills a submissive's fantasy of nonconsensual intercourse.

Fantasy Gang Rape - (See also: Fantasy Rape) Involves the same type of play as Fantasy

Rape with the exception of scene being performed by a group.

Felching – Imbibing semen out of the vagina or anus.

Fellatio - (See also: Head, BJ, Blowjob, Face Fucking) The act of oral sex performed on the penis.

Fellatrix – Someone whose specialty is Fellatio.

Female Domination – Being controlled or lead by a female.

Femdom – A female dominant

Fetish – (See also: kink, paraphilia) Eroticization of an object, body part, style of clothing, etc.; examples of fetishes can be for feet, underwear, latex, leather, etc.

Fetish Attire – Clothes that reflect the wearer's particular fetish, such as leather, latex, rubber or high heels.

Fetishism - Attraction to or tendency toward sexual arousal/behavior/fantasies involving an inanimate object.

Figging – Inserting a piece of fresh, skinless ginger into the rectum, which causes an intense burning sensation.

Financial Domination – Controlling another's financial matters or money.

Finger Flagging – Painting certain fingernails various colors and/or patterns to signify one's erotic preferences. (see Flagging)

Fire Play – (Flame Play) The use of fire in sexual play.

Fisting - Attraction to or tendency toward sexual arousal/behavior/fantasies involving the insertion of a fist into an orifice (vaginal fisting, anal fisting, etc)

Flagellation – BDSM-related whipping, beating and spanking for erotic stimulation.

Flagging- Wearing or displaying a specific color or pattern to signify one's erotic preferences.

Flogger - (See also: Strapping , Whipping) A whip device usually with many "tails". Usually used on the buttocks, back, chest or genital area.

Flogging – using a "flogger" on a submissive.

Flogging horse - A device used to secure and/or restrain the submissive's body for flogging. Usually waist high.

Foley Catheter – Type of catheter that can be inflated with sterile water.

Foot Worship - (See also: Boot Worship , High Heels , Homage , Licking) The practice of play involving a fetish for feet.

Forced Dressing - Forcing the submissive to dress however the Dominant sees fit, whether publicly or privately.

Forced Homosexuality - Scenes where the submissive is forced into sexual relations with someone of the same sex.

Forced Heterosexuality - Scenes where the submissive is forced into sexual relations with someone of the opposite sex.

Forced Lactation – Continual stimulation and sucking of the female nipple can sometimes produce milk. Also known as forced breast milking.

Forced Masturbation - Scenes where the submissive is forced to perform masturbation in front of/for the Dominant or others as a form of erotic / sensual play or humiliation.

Forced Nudity - A scene which involves forcing one's submissive to remain nude either privately or publicly. Generally as a form of control / humiliation. Note: In most areas, this is illegal in public.

Forced Servitude - A form of play involving the submissive acting as a servant / maid to the Dominant. May be played out in public or in private as a form of humiliation.

Forced Smoking - Forcing the submissive to smoke (usually cigarettes); however, other various types of smoking are used in heavy S/m play.

Force-Feeding - A technique by which the Dominant controls the submissive's eating habits.

Formicophilia - Attraction to or tendency toward sexual arousal/behavior/fantasies involving ants.

Freeplay – BDSM play where there is no Domination or submission.

Frotteurism - Attraction to or tendency toward sexual arousal/behavior/fantasies involving rubbing one's genitals against or fondling the body parts of a non-consenting person.

Full-Head Hoods - (See also: Blindfolds) Worn to block the sense of sight for erotic purposes.

Furries – Subculture of people interested in animal play, often dressing in elaborate animal costumes.

G

Gaffer's Tape – see Duct Tape.

Gags – devices used to restrict function or control of the mouth.

Galateism – Sexual attraction to statues.

Gauge – System of measurement and classification by thickness. The lower the number, the thicker the wire or material.

Gay – Primarily refers to a homosexual person or the state of being homosexual.

Gender - the complex interrelationship between an individual's biological sex , one's gender identity or internal sense of self (male, female, both or neither), as well as one's outward presentations and behaviors (gender expression).

Genderfluid - refers to a gender which varies over time or with situational circumstances.

Gender Identity – An indiviual's innermost

concept of self as male or female or both or neither—
how individuals perceive themselves and what they call
themselves. One's gender identity can be the same or
different than the biological sex assigned at birth.

Genderfuck – Practice of transposing different
elements of gender for erotic, political and/or
cultural reasons.

Genderqueer - denoting or relating to a person who
does not subscribe to conventional gender distinctions
but identifies with neither, both, or a combination of
male and female genders.

Genital Sex - To cause an orgasm through
the genital area, done strictly to the genital
area with any body part or through the use of
toys.

Genitorture – Pain play involving the genitals.
(See Ball Torture, Cock and Ball Torture,
Cunt Torture).

Gerontophilla – Preference for sex with the
elderly

Gerontophilia - Attraction to or tendency
toward sexual arousal/behavior/fantasies
involving an elderly partner.

Given Away - Where a Dominant releases a
sub to another Dominant, without exchange
of favors.

Go Down On – Slang term for oral sex (See fellatio, cunnilingus)

Golden Shower – Urination or urine play. Also called piss play, watersports, or WS.

Gun Play - Scenes involving the use of firearms.

Gym Cap – Slang for condom.

Gymnophilia - Attraction to or tendency toward sexual arousal/behavior/fantasies involving nudity.

Gynemimetophilia - Attraction to or tendency toward sexual arousal/behavior/fantasies involving a male impersonating a female.

Gynelophilous - Attraction to or tendency toward sexual arousal/behavior/fantasies involving the sight/touch of pubic hair (see acomoclitic, hirsutophilia, hyphephilia, pubephilia, trichophilia).

H

Haematomania/Hematolagnia - Attraction to or tendency toward sexual arousal/behavior/fantasies involving blood.

Hairbrush Spanking - Play which involves the

use of a hairbrush to inflict pain. Commonly used in "naughty boy / girl" scenes for punishment.

Hair Pulling - Pulling of one's hair for the purpose of pain and/or humiliation.

Hamartophilia - Attraction to or tendency toward sexual arousal/behavior/fantasies involving acts considered to be sinful.

Handcuffs – Common BDSM device used to restrain the wrists.

Hand Job - Using the hands to perform sexual gratification on a man's penis. Stroking of the penis.

Haptephilia - Attraction to or tendency toward sexual arousal/behavior/fantasies involving being touched

Harem – A collection or group of sexual submissives or servants. To have more than one submissive in a scene or in daily life (i.e., the Dominant has a "harem" of women / men). A common occurrence in the Mormon religion, and in polyamorous relationships.

Harness – Elaborate bondage device made with leather straps worn on the body.

Harpaxophilia - Attraction to or tendency

toward sexual arousal/behavior/ fantasies involving being robbed or burglarized (see chrematistophilia).

Head - (See also: Fellatio, Cunnilingus) Slang term for oral sex.

Hedralingus – Licking someone's anus (also called rimming or a rimjob).

Henna – A brown dye made from the leaves of the henna plant. Used in temporary tattoos.

Hierophilia - Attraction to or tendency toward sexual arousal/behavior/fantasies involving objects that are considered sacred.

Hirsutophilia - Attraction to or tendency toward sexual arousal/behavior/fantasies involving armpit hair (see acomoclitic, gynelophilous, hyphephilia, pubephilia, trichophilia).

Homage - (See also: Boot Worship , Foot Worship, Cock Worship) Term meaning to pay respects to; homage; honor. A ceremony involving the submissive "honoring" the Dominant in some way - public or private. Could also mean paying "homage" to the penis / vagina, feet, breasts, etc., by worship.

Hodophilia - Attraction to or tendency toward sexual arousal/behavior/fantasies involving traveling.

Homilophilia - Attraction to or tendency toward sexual arousal/behavior/fantasies involving hearing or giving sermons.

Hood – A head covering, usually made of leather, that the Dominant wears to increase the "fear factor" in a BDSM scene, or that a submissive is made to wear to provide some degree of sensory deprivation.

Horse – In bondage, it is a modification of a sawhorse over which a submissive can be tied. Sometimes called a spanking bench.

Hot Wax - (See also: Waxing) The process of using hot wax in scening. The wax most commonly used are candles and can be used on various parts of the body for erotic stimulation.

Housework - (See also: Chores (Domestic Service)) Play involving the Dominant instructing the submissive to perform domestic duties as a form of punishment / control. Can sometimes also be used as erotic play (i.e., cleaning in the nude).

Humiliation – Most commonly refers to imposing an emotionally/psychologically tense state upon the submissive by requiring them to perform things they normally would not do, most commonly in public (i.e., wearing revealing clothing; having sex in public, etc.).

Hybristophilia - Attraction to or tendency toward sexual arousal/behavior/fantasies involving people who have committed crimes, people who are dangerous/cruel/outrageous.

Hygrophilia - Attraction to or tendency toward sexual arousal/behavior/fantasies involving body fluids or moisture.

Hyphephilia - Attraction to or tendency toward sexual arousal/behavior/fantasies involving touching skin, hair, leather, fur, or fabric/specific fabric (see acomoclitic, doraphilia,gynelophilous, hirsutophilia, pubephilia, trichophilia).

Hypnotism - To place someone in a trance-type state, and offer suggestions into certain types of behavior.

Hypoxyphilia - Attraction to or tendency toward sexual arousal/behavior/fantasies involving the limiting or withholding of oxygen.

I

Iantronudia – Sexual arousal from exposing oneself to a medical doctor.

Ice Play - ice used on nipples or genital areas for desensitization of senses or nerves.

Iconolagny – Sexual arousal from statues depicting nudity.

Immobilization - Any form of bondage technically immobilizes someone; however, this term is usually used for extreme forms of bondage where all body parts are completely restricted from movement. One example is mummification.

Impact Play – BDSM play involving spanking, slapping, beating, or whipping type impact on the body of the submissive with any of various implements including floggers, canes, straps, paddles, bare hand or gloved hand.

Infantilism - Scening where the submissive assumes the role of a child / infant and is treated as such (i.e., diaper wearing, spankings, standing in corner, etc.).

Infibulation – closing off, obstructing or modifying, either permanently or temporarily, the male or female genitalia so as to alter or prevent the conduct of sexual intercourse.

Interrogations - Term meaning question, systematically and formally. Commonly performed in "police interrogations".

Intricate (Japanese) Rope Bondage - (See also: Bondage , Immobilization , Shibari) A very complex form of bondage using rope, usually applied in artful and pleasing patterns.

J

Japanese Clover Nipple Clamps - Type of adjustable nipple clamps that tightens as it is pulled. General preferred because they won't easily slip off.

John – A person who patronizes prostitutes.

K

Kainotophilia - Attraction to or tendency toward sexual arousal/behavior/fantasies involving change.

Kakorrhaphiphilia - Attraction to or tendency toward sexual arousal/behavior/fantasies involving failure.

Keraunophilia - Attraction to or tendency toward sexual arousal/behavior/fantasies involving thunder and/or lightning.

Kidnapping - Term meaning to seize, detain, or carry a person away by unlawful force.

Some players in the BDSM scene have fantasies regarding kidnapping and may ask for a scene involving some sort of "play kidnapping".

Kinesophilia - Attraction to or tendency toward sexual arousal/behavior/fantasies involving exercise.

Kink - Erotic practice or interest which is outside of the mainstream. Also, the word kink is sometimes used interchangeably with Fetish or Paraphilia.

Kink-aware or Kink-friendly - Specifically refers to a vanilla person (See Vanilla) who is informed about and accepting of BDSM and consensual kink.

Kinkphobia - Fearful and/or negative attitudes regarding BDSM, fetish sexuality, kink and/or persons who identify with these orientations; the polar opposite of kink-aware or kink-friendly.

Kinkster - A person who is oriented towards kink, especially one who is openly involved in the kink community at some level.

Kleptophilia - Attraction to or tendency toward sexual arousal/behavior/fantasies involving stealing.

Klismaphilia - Attraction to or tendency toward sexual arousal/behavior/fantasies involving administering or recieving an enema.

Knife Play – A specific form of "edgeplay" where the Dominant uses a knife to either cut or tease the submissive.

Knismolagnia - Attraction to or tendency toward sexual arousal/behavior/fantasies involving tickling or being tickled.

Kolpeuryntomania – Sexual arousal from forced dilation of the vagina.

Kopophilia - Attraction to or tendency toward sexual arousal/behavior/fantasies involving exhaustion.

L

Lactaphilia – Attraction to or tendency toward sexual arousal/behavior/fantasies involving lactating breasts.

Lash – A strike from a whip, paddle, crop or flogger.

Latex Play – Play which uses paint on latex.

Leather – Material made from the cured skin of animals. One of the most popular and widely used of fetish materials; Also many get excited by the look , feel, or smell of leather clothing, boots, etc.

Legcuffs – large handcuffs intended to be used to immobilize or restrict movement of the ankles.

Leg Irons – Steel ankle cuffs. Patterned after British prisoner restraints.

Lingerie - Women's intimate apparel. Lace bodices, stockings, bras, panties, etc.

Limits – Set of limitations which a bottom or submissive sets during negotiation. "Hard limits" are those which should never be crossed, but "soft limits" may change with time, further negotiation, or exploration. Over time a top or dominant may "push limits" to expand the couple's erotic repertoire within a safe, consensual and nurturing context.

Lorum – Piercing through the skin on the underside of the penis.

Lunge Whip – see Quirt.

M

M/s – Master/slave. (Also MS, M&S or M-s)

Ma'am – Term of respect for a female

Dominant.

Macrogenitalism - Attraction to or tendency toward sexual arousal/behavior/fantasies involving unusually large genitals.

Macrophilia - Attraction to or tendency toward sexual arousal/behavior/fantasies involving giants.

Maid – Popular role-play where the submissive dresses and performes as a maid.

Maieusiophilia – Attraction to or tendency toward sexual arousal/behavior/fantasies involving pregnant women.

Malacca – A thick cane.

Maledom, male dom – A male Dominant.

Male Domination – BDSM play where a male is the one in control or who controls the submissive.

Mammagymnophilia – Sexual arousal from female breasts.

Manacles / Irons - (See also: Bondage) Metal rings joined by a chain to restrain the wrist or ankles.

Marks – Temporary or permanent markings

on the skin of a bottom or submissive as a result of consensual play; temporary marks can include bruises, abrasions and cuts; permanent marks can include scarification, tattoos and other body art or body modification.

Martinet – Small flogger.

Masochism - Attraction to or tendency toward sexual arousal/behavior/fantasies involving physical pain, or being dominated/humiliated.

Masochist – One who gets pleasure from pain.

Massage - Using the hands (generally) to massage areas of the body.

Master – Male Dominant, controlling partner in a power exchange relationship, where the submissive partner is known as the slave.

Mastigophilia - Attraction to or tendency toward sexual arousal/behavior/fantasies involving punishment.

Master/Mistress – Both a role and a title frequently assumed by Dominants. A submissive may refer to her/his Dominant as "my Mistress" or "my Master," especially when they have entered a deeper committed relationship.

Medical Scene – BDSM scene involving medical (doctor/patient/nurse) scenarios.

Menophilia – Attraction to or tendency toward sexual arousal/behavior/fantasies involving the female menstrual cycle.

Mentor – A teacher or advisor who often shows a "newbie" around the world of BDSM.

Merinthophilia - Attraction to or tendency toward sexual arousal/behavior/fantasies involving being bound/restrained.

Mindfuck – The practice of making a play partner believe that the course of play is more risky or dangerous than it actually is, as a way of building tension, anticipation and arousal. Psychological trickery.

Mistress – Female Dominant, controlling partner in a power exchange relationship, where the submissive partner is known as the slave.

Mommy – Analogue of Daddy in BDSM play. Sometimes submissives call their Mistress "Mommy."

Mousetraps – Used as a BDSM device for nipple torture. A severe and painful nipple clamp.

Mouth Bits - A type of mouthpiece, generally used on horses and ponies, that is inserted into the mouth and is used to bite down on. Used typically during pony girl / boy play scenes.

Mummification – A unique kind of bondage scene in which the whole body is wrapped tightly in a film – typically plastic wrap.

Munch – Social gathering of kinksters at a restaurant or food court to meet one another, exchange information, etc.; an excellent opportunity for newbies to learn more about their local BDSM community.

Mysophilia - Attraction to or tendency toward sexual arousal/behavior/fantasies involving filth/foul odors/decaying material.

N

Nailing – BDSM play where the scrotum or breasts are nailed to a board.

Narratophilia - Attraction to or tendency toward sexual arousal/behavior/fantasies involving the discussion of sex with others.

Nasogastric tube – Medical device, more commonly known as a feeding tube. Used in control scenes such as forced feeding.

Nasolingus – Sexual arousal from nose sucking.

Nasophilia - Attraction to or tendency toward sexual arousal/behavior/fantasies involving a nose, or noses (see partialism).

Necrochlesis – The act of sex with a corpse.

Necrophilia – Attraction to or tendency toward sexual arousal/behavior/fantasies involving a corpse.

Needle Play – another "edgeplay" where sterilized needles are inserted through the top layer of the skin (the epidermis).

Negotiation – discussing hard and soft limits and related items of BDSM taste before any play or relationship begins. It helps in defining terms of safety and consent between the Dominant and submissive.

Newbie – Novice. In the BDSM/kink/fetish community, this refers to someone not very experienced in kink.

Nipple Clamps – Devices that clamp onto the nipples. Weights can be attached to stretch the nipples. Nipple Clamps often provide increased stimulation which can involve pain and pleasure. See Also, Japanese Clover Nipple Clamps, Alligator Nipple Clamps, Tweezer Nipple Clamps.

Nipple Rings - A ring that is worn through the nipple. Piercing of the nipple and inserting a ring, similar to nose piercing. This type of piercing stimulates the nipple.

Nipple Shield – Decorative nipple jewelry the encircles or even covers the nipple.

Nipple Torture – To cause pain to the nipples. Typically by using nipple clamps, needles, mousetraps, pulling and twisting, etc.

Nipple Weights – Usually weights suspended from either nipple clamps or from nipple piercings.

Novice – see Newbie.

Nyctophilia - Attraction to or tendency toward sexual arousal/behavior/fantasies involving darkness or night.

O

Ochlophilia - Attraction to or tendency toward sexual arousal/behavior/fantasies involving being in a crowd.

Oculolinctus - Attraction to or tendency

toward sexual arousal/behavior/fantasies involving the licking of someone's eyeball

Oculophilia - Attraction to or tendency toward sexual arousal/behavior/fantasies involving eyes (see partialism).

Odaxelagnia - Attraction to or tendency toward sexual arousal/behavior/fantasies involving biting/being bitten.

Odontophilia - Attraction to or tendency toward sexual arousal/behavior/fantasies involving teeth.

Ophidiophilia – Attraction to or tendency toward sexual arousal/behavior/fantasies involving snakes.

Oral Sex – Sex involving contact between mouth and any other sexual organ.

Orgasm – An intense and explosive discharge of neuromuscular tensions at the height of sexual arousal that is usually accompanied by the ejaculation of semen by the male and by vaginal contractions in the woman.

Orientation – In the context of the BDSM/kink/fetish community, "orientation" can take many meanings beyond one's gender-based attraction, such as their preferred role (see bottom, Dominant, submissive, switch, and top). Also, many kinksters regard their BDSM/kink/fetish sexuality to be a sexual/affectional orientation.

Orogastric Tube – A tube from mouth to stomach. Used in force feeding scenes.

Osphresiolagnia – Sexual arousal from foul smells.

OTK – "Over the Knee" spanking- were the subject is placed over the lap of the person administering the spanking.

Outdoor Scenes - Scenes involving the great outdoors! Any scene where the action is outside during scening.

Ozolagnia - Attraction to or tendency toward sexual arousal/behavior/fantasies involving powerful scents.

P

PA – see Prince Albert.

Paddle – A flat instrument used for spanking purposes; usually made of wood or some other rigid material.

Padlock – Common type of lock used in BDSM play. Use to secure bondage restraints, securely fasten chain links together, as labia weights, etc.

Pain – Pain causes the release of endorphins that is thought causes the submissive to go into subspace.

Pain Games – BDSM play involving pain.

Pain Slut – Popular expression for a submissive who loves pain. Also a masochist.

Pain Threshold – The point, unique for each individual, at which stimulation becomes too painful to reasonably bear.

Pansexual (Pansexuality) – Encompassing all gender identities and sexual/affectional orientations.

Parachute (also Parachute Ball Stretcher)- Round leather device which is fitted between the scrotum and the base of the penis, usually with chains for weights to be added.

Parachute Ball Stretcher – A round leather device resembling a parachute, which is fitted between the scrotum and the base of the penis. Includes chains or other attaching points from which weights can be suspended in ball torture scenes.

Parthenophilia - Attraction to or tendency

toward sexual arousal/behavior/fantasies involving sex with virgins.

Partialism - Attraction to or tendency toward sexual arousal/behavior/fantasies involving specific parts of the body(see alvinolagnia, nasophilia, oculophilia, podophilia).

PE – see Power Exchange.

Pecattiphilia - Attraction to or tendency toward sexual arousal/behavior/fantasies involving sinning/guilt.

Pediophilia - Attraction to or tendency toward sexual arousal/behavior/fantasies involving dolls.

Permanent Piercing – Piercing the body in order to insert jewelry that is intended to be worn on at least a semi-permanent basis.

Phallophilia - Attraction to or tendency toward sexual arousal/behavior/fantasies involving a large penis.

Phobophilia - Attraction to or tendency toward sexual arousal/behavior/fantasies involving fear and/or hate.

Phone Sex - Play which involves having simulated sex or masturbation over the telephone. Some phone companies deem this illegal.

Piercing - Piercing of the body with a thin sharp object such as a needle. There are two types: permanent and temporary. Permanent piercing is done with a thicker needle which enables jewelry to be easily inserted. Temporary piercing (see also Play Piercing) is done with a smaller, thinner needle which can be removed without permanent scarring after the session is completed.

Piss Play – see Water Sports, Golden Showers.

Play – BDSM or kink activity. Also used to refer to specific interests (age play, animal play, impact play, etc.).

Play Party – A social gathering where people may engage in or observe demonstrations of BDSM play.

Play Piercing – Piercing the body temporarily. All piercings are removed at the end of the session.

Plushophilia - Attraction to or tendency toward sexual arousal/behavior/fantasies involving stuffed toys.

Podophilia - Attraction to or tendency toward sexual arousal/behavior/fantasies involving feet (see Partialism).

Pony Play – Role-play scene where the submissive takes on the role of a pony.

Polyamory – Consensual non-monogamy. (See Swinging)

Polyiterophilia - Attraction to or tendency toward sexual arousal/behavior/fantasies involving sexual acts with a series of partners.

Pony gear – Gear intended specifically for pony play. May include hoods, bits (for mouth), bridles, straps, harnesses, saddles and anal plug tails. Some use hoof shoes as well.

Power Exchange – The dynamic whereby the Dominant (Top) is consensually given power over the submissive (bottom), whether for just the scene or for a relationship. Sometimes called Total Power Exchange or TPE.

Press Style Nipple Clamps – These are nipple clamps that press the nipple between two pieces of metal usually forced together by a thumb screw.

Prince Albert – Also known as a PA. A male piercing between the urethra and the underside of the penis. Not named after the

Prince of Monaco.

Prison Scening - Acting out a scene involving prison. The use of a *cell* is for punishment and humiliation.

ProDomme (ProDom) –(female and male) Shorthand terms for a professional Dominant. A Dominant who provides BDSM sessions for paid clientele. More commonly female, but there are some male professional Dominants also.

Prostitution - The selling or renting of one's body for sexual uses or purposes (i.e., selling sex or sexual favors).

Protocol – The rules of conduct, ritual and etiquette within (a) a specific D/s relationship, (b) a BDSM play party or club, or (c) the larger BDSM/kink/fetish community. While there are both regional and subcultural variations, protocol is generally based upon ideas of safety and respect.

Psychrocism - Attraction to or tendency toward sexual arousal/behavior/fantasies involving cold/ice.

Pubephilia - Attraction to or tendency toward sexual arousal/behavior/fantasies involving pubic hair (see acomoclitic, gynelophilous, hirsutophilia, hyphephilia, trichophilia).

Public Exposure - Play which involves exposing oneself (usually genitals) in public (i.e., flashing).

Punishment - Scenes where the Dominant "punishes" the submissive.

Puppy Play – Perhaps the most popular of animal RPGs. Here, the submissive actually mimics a puppy.

Pussy Torture – The use of BDSM devices – such as clamps – on the female gential area to produce pain.

Pussy Whipping – Striking the area with different types of equipment (i.e., floggers, crops, slappers, etc.) for erotic pleasure.

Pussy Worship - The practice of erotic play involving the "worship" of the female genitalia. Scenes may involve cleaning, licking, shaving, etc.

Pygmalianism – Attraction to or tendency toward sexual arousal/behavior/fantasies involving sex with statues or inanimate objects.

Pygophilia - Attraction to or tendency toward sexual arousal/behavior/fantasies involving contact with the buttocks.

Pyrophilia - Attraction to or tendency toward sexual arousal/behavior/fantasies involving fire.

Q

Quirt – A type of buggy whip used for whipping the submissive.

R

Rack - A table-like device (patterned after the torture device of the same name used during the Spanish Inquisition) which is fitted with pulling or stretching capabilities. Some racks incorporate pulleys, winches or wheels for pulling one in opposing directions.

Real Life or Real Time – r/l or r/t – as opposed to virtual, online or cyber life.

Religious Scene - A form of play usually clerical attire and roleplay.

Restraint – Limiting the bottom's movement with the use of various bondage gear, equipment or devices.

Restriction – Limiting the bottom's behavior or physical movement.

Retifism - Attraction to or tendency toward

sexual arousal/behavior/fantasies involving shoes (see altocalciphilia).

Rhabdophilia - Attraction to or tendency toward sexual arousal/behavior/fantasies involving being flagellated.

Riding Crop - A short whip-type instrument made of leather with a "loop" at the end which is intended for use on horses.

Rimming - (See also: Anal Play) Mouth contact with the rectal area, which may include insertion of the tongue.

Ring Gag – A device that keeps the submissive's mouth wide open.

Risk-Aware Consensual Kink (RACK) – An alternate formulation for BDSM's ethos, considered a more realistic and/or inclusive maxim compared to Safe, Sane and Consensual (SSC).

Robotism - Attraction to or tendency toward sexual arousal/behavior/fantasies involving robots.

Roleplay, Role Play, Role-Play, Role Play Games, RPG – Adopting roles (characters, personae, different gender identities, dominant or submissive stances) within an erotic context, to enhance arousal, give context to specific forms of play (i.e., caning and other punishment within a "teacher/student" role-play) and/or added fun.

Rope – The most common of bondage equipment.

RPG – See Roleplay.

Rubber – After leather, the most popular fetish material.

S

S&M – Sadism and masochism. Generally, the Sadist enjoys administering pain, and the masochist enjoys recieving pain.

Sadism - Attraction to or tendency toward sexual arousal/behavior/fantasies involving humiliating or inflicting pain upon one's partner.

Sadist – An individual who enjoys causing pain. The term dates back to the Marquis de Sade.

Sadomasochism – Tendency toward taking pleasure, especially sexual gratification, from inflicting and/or receiving pain or other intense stimuli.

Safe-Call – Arrangement for assuring a person's safety when meeting someone for BDSM play; the person arranges to call a "safe-call buddy" at a prearranged time, and if the buddy does not receive the call, the buddy then contacts the police or makes other arrangements to ensure the safety of the person.

Safe, Sane, and Consensual (SSC) – Maxim within the BDSM/kink/fetish community, delineating acceptable forms of play. While the expanded meaning of these terms is still discussed and disputed within the Scene, the general consensus is: (a) "Safe" means not causing injury which would require professional intervention to heal; (b) "Sane" means being able to distinguish fantasy from reality; (c) "Consensual" means that all activity taking place is understood and agreed to by all who are involved.

Safe Word – A previously agreed upon word, phrase or signal a submissive can use to stop his or her scene. It is absolute and non-negotiable. If a Dominant disregards a submissive's safe word, that Dominant is acting without consent. The most common safe word is "RED!" Some also use a caution word such as "Yellow" to signify that the dominant is approaching a limit.

Safe Sex – Using condoms and taking all necessary precautions against the spread of STD's and/or unwanted pregnancy during sex.

Saint Andrews Cross - This is a cross made in an X formation. It is generally angled and self-supporting. Some are suspended from ceilings, or mounted directly to a wall. The cross has restraints for arms, legs and body. Salirophilia - Attraction to or tendency toward sexual arousal/behavior/fantasies involving ingesting human sweat or saliva (fluids with a salt content).

SAM – Smart Ass Masochist. A pseudo submissive who generally attempts to assert control from the role of bottom.

Scat – Fecal matter, or play which involves fecal matter. An abbreviation for "scatological."

Scatophilia- Attraction to or tendency toward sexual arousal/behavior/fantasies involving fecal matter.

Scene – A BDSM session, also known as a play session. May refer to a "public scene" at a party where the participants let others watch, or a "private scene" where just the participants are present. "The Scene" is also used to refer to the BDSM/kink/fetish community, or a specific subgroup within it (i.e., "the Gorean Scene").

Schoolgirl Role-play – Popular RPG wherein the submissive is the "school girl".

Scratching - Scratching the body with the fingernails or another instrument for mild pain. (See also: Abrasion)

Self-Bondage – The practice of performing bondage on oneself by oneself.

Sensation Play – Erotic play involving the use of various techniques of sensory stimulation and/or deprivation.

Sensory Deprivation - Play which involves "depriving" the submissive of certain sensory perceptions. May include blindfolds, bondage, gags, confinement, etc.

Service Top – A top who engages in play at the direction of the bottom. For example, a Sadist who administers pain at the direction of a masochist.

Sex Radical – Term for politically active members of the alt-sex community, especially those who seek to challenge laws and cultural norms which discriminate against alternative lifestyles and sexual minorities.

Shackle – Metal or leather bondage restraint device consisting of round cuffs joined by a chain or bar.

Shibari - (See also: Bondage , Intricate Japanese Rope Bondage) The art of Intricate Japanese Rope Bondage. Bondage patterns are intricate and artistically pleasing.

Single-Tail – The classic snakelike whip, shorter ones being called signal whips and longer ones bullwhips.

Sitophilia - Attraction to or tendency toward sexual arousal/behavior/fantasies involving food.

Skinny Dipping – The act of swimming in the nude.

Slapper – A paddle modified to make a loud sound.

Slave – A term used interchangeably with "submissive." Many consider a slave a more extreme version of a submissive.

Slave Contract – A signed consensual contract, wherein a submissive or slave releases and transfers to the Dom or Master a specified set of powers for a set period of time.

Somnophilia - Attraction to or tendency toward sexual arousal/behavior/fantasies involving fondling a stranger in their sleep.

Sound – Medical device designed to be inserted into the urethra. Used in medical play. The act is called urethral sounding.

Spanking - (See also: Beating) involves striking someone with the palm of the hand or other object (i.e., paddle, hairbrush, pig slapper, riding crop, etc.). Used as both punishment, humuliation, and/or in role-play context in BDSM scenes.

Spectrophilia - Attraction to or tendency toward sexual arousal/behavior/fantasies involving spirits, ghosts, or ethereal beings.

Speculum - A medical instrument (usually made of steel or plastic and in the shape of a duckbill) intended for the use of medical examination of the vagina or rectum. The speculum is lubricated and inserted. After insertion, the "bill" is spread apart to open the orifice being examined.

Spencer Paddle – Type of wooden paddle with holes drilled though it.

Spreader Bar – A long metal rod designed to hold the submissive/bottom's legs, thighs or even wrists apart.

Stigmatophilia – Sexual attraction to those with body modifications such as piercings, brands, scars, tattoos.

Stigmatophilia - Attraction to or tendency toward sexual arousal/behavior/fantasies involving the marking a body or insertion of foreign objects into it (tattoos, piercings, etc), or tendency for arousal/attraction toward those who posess such body modifications.

Stocks – A piece of bondage furniture patterned after the Puritan model. The head and hands go through holes while the submissive is standing, bent at the waist.

Straight Jacket - (See also: Bondage) A type of restraint. A jacket type of garment meant to be worn "backwards", consisting of close-ended sleeves that are strapped crisscrossed around the back and tied or locked in place.

Strangling – see Breath Control.

Strapon – A harness (worn around the waist) with a dildo (see Dildo) attached in a somewhat anatomically correct orientation.

Sub – see Submissive.

Subby – see Submissive.

Subbie – see Submissive.

Submissive- One who cedes power to another in a power exchange. One who bends to the will and desire of another (usually called the Top or Dominant), usually within negotiated limits.

Submission – The act of submitting to the will and desire of another (usually called the Top or Dominant), usually within negotiated limits.

Submissive Sadist - A top who enjoys delivering erotic pain or other intense sensation at the direction of the bottom.

Sub-Space - A euphoric state experienced by some submissives and bottoms during play scenes. Also referred to as bottom-space or endorphin high

Surface Burn – A temporary brand, usually produced with heated copper wire.

Surface Piercing – Temporary piercing through the skin's surface.

Suspension – suspending a submissive with ropes, webbing or chain so that no part of the body touches the floor.

Swapping - The "swapping" of one's partner

generally for sexual or erotic play. Switching partners temporarily for play purposes. (See also: Swinging, Polyamory)

Switch – A person who alternates between the role of top and bottom, and/or dominant and submissive, depending upon various contexts (play partners, types of play, etc.).

Symphorophilia - Attraction to or tendency toward sexual arousal/behavior/fantasies involving a crash/disaster/explosion.

T

Tantalolagnia - Attraction to or tendency toward sexual arousal/behavior/fantasies involving teasing.

Taphephilia - Attraction to or tendency toward sexual arousal/behavior/fantasies involving being buried alive.

Tattoo - (See also: Branding) A permanent form of scarring to the body in the form of various types of pictures or drawings or names, etc. Also sometimes used as a permanent form of "marking the submissive" as property.

Teasing - The act of "teasing" to enhance erotic play or pleasure.

Temporary Piercing – Piercing the body temporarily. All piercings are removed at the end of the session. Same as play piercing.

TENS Unit - (See also: Electricity , Violet Wand) Term meaning Transcutaneous Electrical Neural Stimulation unit. A machine designed to apply electrical impulses to specific body tissues at safe levels.

Teratophilia - Attraction to or tendency toward sexual arousal/behavior/fantasies involving deformed or monstrous people (see dysmorphophilia).

Thesauromania - Attraction to or tendency toward sexual arousal/behavior/fantasies involving collecting women's clothing.

Thlipsosis - Attraction to or tendency toward sexual arousal/behavior/fantasies involving pinching.

Thumb Cuffs - Restraining devices designed to restrain the thumbs.

Tickling - Tickling the body to induce laughter.

Timophilia - Attraction to or tendency toward sexual arousal/behavior/fantasies involving gold or wealth (see chrysophilia).

Trainer – Usually a Dominant who helps submissives understand various aspects of the kink/BDSM lifestyle.

Triple Penetration - Penetration of the body by three objects or body parts simultaneously. Example: Insertion of the penis, dildo, butt plug in a female submissive all at once to enhance sexual stimulation.

Top – A Dominant, the person in the power exchange who has been given control and/or authority, and usually the person who delivers instruction, sensation, and/or restraint to a consenting bottom during play.

Topping from the Bottom – Practice of assuming a bottom or submissive role, but directing the top or dominant. Once seen negatively, but now recognized as a legitimate form of play in some circumstances, such as when a seasoned bottom guides a novice top. See also dominant masochist, service top, submissive sadist.

Torture – To cause pain or distress with a specific goal in mind. Usually connotates both a physical and psychological impact on the one being tortured.

Total Power Exchange (TPE) – Alternate term for lifestyle D/s; also sometimes referred to as 24/7.

Toy – Any piece of equipment used during BDSM play: floggers, bondage equipment, vibrators, etc. Sometimes submissives may playfully refer to themselves as the "toy" of their respective dominant.

TPE – (see Total Power Exchange).

Transformation fetish - Attraction to or tendency toward sexual arousal/behavior/fantasies involving depictions of transformations of people into objects/other beings.

Transgender (Transgenderism) – posessing some aspects (mannerisms, behaviors, appearance, tastes etc) of the opposite sex while still maintaining some of the above of your biological sex.

Transsexual - a person having a strong desire to assume the physical characteristics and gender role of the opposite sex.

Trichophilia - Attraction to or tendency toward sexual arousal/behavior/fantasies involving hair. (see also: acomoclitic, gynelophilous, hirsutophilia, hyphephilia, pubephilia).

Tripsolagnophilia - Attraction to or tendency toward sexual arousal/behavior/fantasies involving massage.

Tweezer Nipple Clamps – A style of nipple clamp that resembles a pair of tweezers with a ring around the outside. As you push the ring toward the pincher ends, it causes the clamp to tighten.

U

Uniform – Articles of clothing usually used in roleplaying. Uniforms could include cheerleader uniform, maid uniform, etc.

Urethral Play - (See also: Catheterization, Sound, Urethral Sound) Play involving the "urethra", the tube that runs between the bladder and the outside of the body. In men, it emerges at the end of the penis, and in women, just inside the vagina.

Urethral Sound – Medical device designed to be inserted into the urethra. In BDSM context, it is used in medical roleplay.

Urolagnia – Attraction to or tendency toward sexual arousal/behavior/fantasies involving urine or the act of urination.

Urtication - Attraction to or tendency toward sexual arousal/behavior/fantasies involving stinging nettles stimulating the skin.

V

Vaccinophilia - Attraction to or tendency toward sexual arousal/behavior/fantasies involving being vaccinated or recieving a similar injection.

Vacuum Pumping – Using the suction of a vacuum during play. Generally applied to erogenous zones or sensitive body parts.

Vanilla – People not involved in the BDSM or Fetish lifestyle.

Vibrator - (See also: Anal plug , Dildo) A device made in varying shapes and sizes and powered by either battery or plug-in electrical type. Used as a form of genital stimulation (most commonly for women) to enhance arousal and/or promote orgasm. (Note: Cleopatra of Egypt owned a vibrator. This was a gourd-type hollow object with a small hole and a cork-like plug. It is believed that bees were placed inside and then agitated (shaken) to provide the vibration.)

Vicarphilia - Attraction to or tendency toward sexual arousal/behavior/fantasies involving hearing stories about other people's lives.

Vincilagnia - Attraction to or tendency toward sexual arousal/behavior/fantasies involving one's partner being bound/restrained/tied up.

Violet Wand - (See also: Electricity, TENS Unit) A device used commonly in electrical type play which discharges energy when touched to the body.

Virtual life or Virtual Time – v/l or v/t – often used to describe "online life" as opposed to r/l (real life).

Vorarephilia - Attraction to or tendency toward sexual arousal/behavior/fantasies involving being swallowed or eaten alive.

Voyeurism - Attraction to or tendency toward sexual arousal/behavior/fantasies involving watching others.

W

Water Sports – The practice of urine play. Also called Golden Showers (or GS).

Water Torture – Includes various forms of torture involving water.

Waxing - Using warmed wax as a form of erotic sensation.

Wax Play – Erotic play in which the Dominant applies hot wax the submissive's skin.

Weights – Used to stretch body parts such as nipples, scrotum and labia; usually attached to clamps or piercings.

Whip – Device used in whipping. Usually made of leather.

Whipping - (See also: Caning , Flogger , Strapping)Whipping the body with a whip type device.

Whipping Post - Designs vary according to builder, but the principle is to have a tall post with tethers that hang down, to attach a person from their wrists. Used for exposing and positioning a submissive for ease of whipping.
WIITWD – Acronym for "What It Is That We Do"; an alternative term for BDSM / kink.

X

Xenophilia - Attraction to or tendency toward sexual arousal/behavior/fantasies involving strangers.

Z

Zelophilia - Attraction to or tendency toward sexual arousal/behavior/fantasies involving jealousy.